TORONTO

JOSEF HANUS & JOSEF M. HANUS

Personal gift to:

From:

Toronto…

The northwest shore of Lake Ontario is home to Toronto, Canada's largest industrial and business community, and the capital city of Ontario. Toronto is situated in the southern part of the province. The site was originally a native settlement, and French colonists started fur trading here. Fort York was then established here in 1793. The old garrison was destroyed and rebuilt after American occupations in 1830. The colony, with ten thousand inhabitants, was incorporated in 1834 as the city of Toronto. Today, the city and its environs are populated by almost 5 million people in an area of 632 square kilometres. This early morning picture of the Toronto skyline was taken from Smith Park in Etobicoke.

...A Meeting Place

The name Toronto comes from native language and means, "a meeting place." This is a very suitable and accurate expression especially for this city; Toronto has always been the most important meeting place in Canada. Most Canadian business meetings, government occasions and official international visits are held in Toronto's congress halls, downtown offices, and hotels. Toronto is the first destination of ninety percent of all tourists visiting Canada, over 21 million people annually. An interesting historic fact is that the first meeting on this site was between explorer Etienne Brules and the Andaste nation in 1615. On page 82 is a picture of the park surrounding the Humber River by the Old Mill Bridge, named for Etienne Brule. The two photographs on this page are common views of the Toronto downtown, taken on King Street West, and Front Street West.

Fort York

This oldest part of Toronto was established by Lt. Gov. John Graves Simcoe, a veteran of the American Revolution in 1793, to guard the young city from the lake side. In 1812–13, Fort York was twice captured by the Americans. One year later, Canadian and British troops resisted an invading force of 1700 Americans. In 1830, Fort York was rebuilt and now serves as a museum of an era past, with scarlet-coated guardsmen, old powder magazines, barracks, a six pounder cannon and office quarters. Fort York is considered to be the birthplace of modern Toronto.

Fort Rouillé

More recently known as Fort Toronto, the last French post was erected on this site in 1750. The fort was established by order of the Marquis de la Jonquière to help strengthen French control of the Great Lakes. Fort Rouillé was destroyed in 1759.

Bloor Street

Splitting Toronto North–South, Bloor Street is one of the oldest and most popular streets in the city. Some of the city's most well known places, such as the Colonnade, Bata Shoe Museum, Honest Ed's stores, Chapters, Public Library, Royal Ontario Museum and more are situated by Bloor Street or within its neighbourhood.

Little Trinity

Toronto's oldest surviving church, the Little Trinity Anglican Church, is located near the Enoch Turner Schoolhouse. The schoolhouse, pictured on page 32, can be found on Trinity Street, just metres from the church, which is located on 425 King Street East.

University of Toronto

Founded in 1827 as King's College by British Royal Charter, the University of Toronto is the largest complex of university colleges in Canada. Toronto's St. George campus at the university's centre is located between Bloor and College Streets. University College and Trinity College, constructed in Gothic–Victorian style are featured on this page. For tourists and visitors there are three daily organised tours of the campus.

Queen's Park Avenue

The Department of Household Science can be seen in the smaller picture.

Convocation Hall

Thousands of graduating students, followed by their families and faculty members, pass through the Convocation Hall every spring and fall. All 1700 places in the Convocation Hall are usually occupied during graduation. On this page we see a student graduation in Convocation Hall on King's College Circle. 55,000 students, faculty and staff occupy over 100 university buildings on three campuses, located in Toronto, Mississauga and Scarborough. The University of Toronto has 86 doctoral programs, 14 professional faculties and 20 affiliated teaching hospitals. The University library, "Robarts Library" pictured on page 9, houses 12.8 million volumes.

Graduation

The interior of the Convocation Hall was photographed during the spring graduation.

Hart House

A unique social and cultural facility and a gift to the university from the Massey Foundation, Hart House was named after Hart Massey. The building is located in the centre of the university area and first opened in 1919. The Hart House serves students and the public with two main functions—cultural programs and athletic activities. 32 clubs and committees, with weekly events, restaurants and guest rooms are open to visitors. The independently run historic Hart House Theatre offers to its visitors and patrons an annual Drama Festival, Film Festival, Festival of Dance and more.

Stewart Observatory

The Stewart Observatory and The Soldiers Tower (Memorial Tower), located by the Hart House on Hart Tower Road.

Toronto Library

The Toronto Reference Library, the head of the largest public library system in Canada, is located in Yorkville by Yonge Street. It was created on January 1, 1998, when the former library systems of Etobicoke, Scarborough, East and North York, Metro Reference Library and York merged to become the New Toronto Public Library. Daily, thousands of people access information from the library's 11 million items, across 98 branches. Sunday hours, home and hospital delivery, and special services for people with disabilities are just a few of the public services offered. Its unique collections offer visitors information on Native Peoples, Consumer Health Information Services, Gateway Services, and more. Electronic books are also becoming very popular. The building, which also houses a Performing Arts Centre, was designed by Moriyama and Teshima Architects and opened in 1978.

University Library

The third picture shows Robarts University Library, located on St. George Street. This library has 12.8 million volumes.

The Grange

Home to the Art Gallery of Ontario in 1900–1917, an English style manor named The Grange was built in 1817. Renovated to emulate the style of 1830, the Grange Historic House re-opened to the public in 1973. The oldest remaining brick house in Toronto, it was willed to the Gallery around 1911, and is still an integral part of the AGO. The building is located on Dundas Street, just behind the Art Gallery of Ontario. The entrance is seen here from the park by Grange Street.

Victoria University

Originally founded in Cobourg in 1829, Victoria University was relocated to Toronto in 1890. In this picture is Emmanuel College, located in Queen's Park Crescent East. Emmanuel College is the theological department of Victoria University at the University of Toronto.

Bloor St.–Avenue Rd.

Famous for its chamber and vocal music of the French Baroque period, the Church of the Redeemer is located on the intersection of Bloor Street and Avenue Road. Here, worshippers can experience performances from the Musicians In Ordinary, of its Advent vespers from 17th century Venice, Italian madrigalists and other inspiring concerts. The church's Eden London Price Memorial Chapel is decorated with the symbols of the reredos. The reredos were based on the Service of the Litany found in the Prayer Book.

The Colonnade

The Colonnade was built on Bloor Street in 1960. The Colonnade was Canada's first project combining theatre, restaurants, offices and stores with apartments. Also shown in the picture is a three–storey Chapters store, part of Canada's largest bookstore chain.

11

Spadina House

This magnificent mansion was built in 1866 on the bluff above Spadina Avenue. The Victorian house was the home of James Austin, the first president of The Toronto Dominion Bank. The family moved out in 1982 and left the building to the Historical Board of Toronto. Guided visitors can see the ten rooms out of 35 open to the public, its impressive interior, fine furnishings collected over three generations, and the six–acre garden.

Toronto Archives

The City of Toronto Archives are located on Spadina Road, close to Casa Loma and Spadina House. The Archives, which feature exhibits, films and demonstrations, were completed in 1992. People can submit private documents or photographs to the Archives for restoration or conservation.

Casa Loma

Toronto's castle is nestled on the hill overlooking the city from the north. A sample of European architectural elegance, Casa Loma was built in 1911 by the prominent Toronto financier, industrialist and military man, Sir Henry M. Pellatt. This unusual building was designed by the architect J.E. Lennox, the man responsible for Toronto's Old City Hall. As well as its 98 rooms, Casa Loma has 22 fireplaces. The building was constructed in three years by 300 workers and cost 3.5 million dollars. Casa Loma, a favourite tourist destination, is now owned by the City of Toronto and operated by the Kiwanis Club of Casa Loma. One event this summer was an exhibit showcasing the dramatic transformation of women's fashions in the first decades of the last century, named The Dawn of Fashion Freedom. After a tour in historically furnished interiors, visitors can enjoy the brilliant floral mosaic of the all–season gardens.

Riverdale

Riverdale Farm and surrounding Riverdale Park is a lovely weekend destination. Riverdale Park is located by Cabbagetown, between Parliament Street and Bayview Avenue in the southern part of the Don Valley. Nearby are the St. James Cemetery, Wellsley Park and the historic Necropolis Cemetery.

Necropolis

Necropolis Chapel, the entrance to one of Toronto's oldest nonsectarian cemeteries, is among the finest examples of Gothic Revival architecture in Canada. The old cemetery is the final resting place for many of Toronto's premier citizens and pioneers, such as the city's first mayor William L. Mackenzie, the founder of the Globe and Mail newspaper George Brown, and others. The Necropolis was designed by Henry Langley and opened in 1872.

Rosedale

Attractive and expensive, built mainly from stone and brick, old houses settled in beautiful old–fashioned gardens can be seen around the streets of Rosedale, Toronto's luxury district. This romantic area located north of downtown is surrounded by D. Balfour Park and by Don Valley Brick Works Park.

Don Valley

The green space flanking the Don River spreads some five kilometres from Flemington Park on the north to Riverdale Park on the south. It is a complex of parks and recreational zones located in the centre of East York. The most well known areas are Don Valley Brick Works Park, Thorncliffe Park with its Greek Cultural Centre, and Riverdale Park.

Colborne Lodge

Nestled in High Park, Colborne Lodge was the residence of John George Howard. He arrived in Canada in 1832 and settled in the town of York. Sir John Colborne hired Mr. Howard as Drawing Master at the College and later, John Howard was made City Surveyor in 1843. Built in 1837, this rare picturesque Regency villa is a graceful monument to the founders of Toronto's largest park: J.G. Howard and his wife Jemima.

Sunnyside

Sunnyside Amusement Park and its facilities, the Club Esquire, Palais Royale, Merry-Go-Round, Derby Racer and the Flyer roller-coaster, opened in 1922. A fire destroyed the park in November 1955. Several buildings remained, of which the Palais Royale and Bathing Pavilion were renovated and officially rededicated in 1980.

Montgomery's Inn

Located on Dundas Street, historic Montgomery's Inn was built in 1830. Originally the home of Irish immigrant Thomas Montgomery, the building is now restored as an 1840's museum.

Art Gallery of Ontario

The Art Gallery of Ontario, Canada's second largest art museum, was founded in 1900 and today holds one of Canada's most extensive collections of fine art. The European collection is popular, as is the Henry Moore Centre, the Inuit collection, the Canadian collection, Contemporary art and more. The holding includes work of some the world's most famous artists: Degas, Picasso, Rembrandt, Durer, Gauguin and Matisse. The Canadian collection also has a room dedicated to the Group of Seven. The large photograph shows the Georgia Ridley Gallery, known as The Salon Gallery, which features works by Canadian artists from the 19th century. The AGO is at 317 Dundas St. W, where it has been since its original building, The Grange, was willed to the Gallery in 1911. The modern facade dates from 1990. Large Two Forms, a bronze sculpture by Henry Moore, is a well known landmark by the entrance.

Cabbagetown

British residents who lived in the area in the 1860's planted vegetables, mostly cabbages, in their front gardens. From this habit came the name of this lovely Toronto neighbourhood. Colourful brick and wood Victorian homes with well maintained old–fashioned flower gardens give the area a charming appearance. Cabbagetown is located by Riverdale Park and Don Valley. Nearby are Riverdale Farm and Necropolis Cemetery with its picturesque chapel. A trip to this area can be combined with a visit to the Allan Gardens on Sherbourne and Carlton Street East. (page 74.)

Dundas Street

St. Patricks Church by the intersection of Dundas and McCaul Streets.

Yorkville

Originally a suburb, Yorkville became part of Toronto in 1883. Its Victorian houses were converted into art galleries, cozy restaurants, pubs and fashionable boutiques. Today's Yorkville is sought out by tourists and Torontonians as a haven to a bygone era.

Fire Hall

Yorkville's oldest Fire Hall was built in 1876. The Fire Hall, still in service, is a popular Toronto tourist attraction. In addition to this site, it is nice to visit other historical places such as Black Creek Village, Scarborough Historical Museum, Montgomery's Inn, Todmorden Mills, Gibson House, The Market Gallery, or Colborne Lodge.

Toronto Markets

St. Lawrence Market and farmers' markets located on Front Street in the St. Lawrence district are a preferred shopping destination for locals. Other well known markets are Kensington, Chinatown, Little Italy, Little India and Greektown. Numerous ethnic restaurants and colourful stores, nestled under historic houses, offer everything from vegetables, oriental spices, fabrics, live fish and expensive antiques.

Chinatown

The busy Chinese community is located by Spadina and Dundas streets. Every doorway offers smells and sights that hail from the other side of the globe. Vegetables, fruit, fish, spices and ethnic dishes give this neighbourhood an exotic smell. Exhausted by the busy downtown, tourists can relax while browsing tasteful stores and stylish cafés. Another romantic area close to Kensington Market is Little Italy, on College Street.

Gardiner Museum

An interesting collection of ceramic and plastic artwork can be viewed at the Gardiner Museum of Ceramic Art, located on Queen's Park Avenue. Toronto has numerous interesting museums such as the Haïda Naval Museum, Toronto Police Museum, Children's Own Museum, Bata Shoe Museum, Zion Schoolhouse, CBC Museum, North York Fire Dept. Museum and more. Pictures from the Royal Ontario Museum are on page 24.

Design Exchange

A part of Toronto's history is the former Toronto Stock Exchange Building, named the Design Exchange. The building, located on 234 Bay Street, is occasionaly open to the public. The new Toronto Stock Exchange building is found on King and York Streets.

University Avenue

Toronto's widest boulevard connects middletown with Queen's Park and the Ontario Legislature Building. Princess Margaret Hospital, The Toronto Hospital, Goverment buildings and Osgoode Hall are all located on University Avenue. The Ontario Parliament Buildings are nestled at the very northern end of University Avenue.

War Cenotaph

This monument to the memory of the Canadians who died defending the British Empire in the South African War in 1899–1902 is placed on University Avenue by Osgoode Hall and Queen Street West. The creator of this 1909 sculpture is Walter S. Allward.

Ontario Parliament

The Richardsonian Romanesque building has been the meeting place for the provincial legislature for over 100 years. The building, which dominates the north end of University Avenue and Dundas Street, was designed by architect Richard A. Waite. The statues of famous public figures, including Queen Victoria and Canada's first Prime Minister, John A. Macdonald, stand in the park in front of the building.

Canada Day

A big cake decorated with a Canadian Flag is traditionally offered on July 1 to participants of the Canada Day celebration in front of the Ontario Parliament. Numerous events for children and families are provided all day long to Torontonians in Queen's Park. Canada Day is very popular and celebrated by thousands.

Royal Ontario Museum

The Royal Ontario Museum (ROM) is located on Queen's Park Ave., close to Bloor Street. This is the most visited museum in Toronto. The ROM holds huge collections of fine and applied art, archaeology and natural sciences. Thirteen dinosaur skeletons draw children and adults into the intimately illuminated Dinosaur Gallery. A large collection of Egyptian Mummies, a Jamaican Bat Cave, Chinese galleries and more are a draw for hundreds of school groups. ROM, the largest museum in Canada, opened on May 12, 1914—on the same day the S.S. Titanic sank east of Newfoundland. A magnificent gold ceiling in the entrance is the first wonder to be seen by visitors. It represents the fine architecture of this early 20th century building. The second photo shows the building, frequently visited by school trips from around Ontario. The building was built first to house collections from Toronto University.

Osgoode Hall

Osgoode Hall and its well maintained park has been the hub of legal life in Ontario for more than 170 years. The name honours W. Osgoode, the first Chief Justice of the province. The Supreme Court Of Justice, the Court of Appeal for Ontario and the Law Society of Upper Canada currently reside at Osgoode Hall, which is a National Historic Site and one of the most beautiful buildings in Canada.

Nathan Phillips Square

The second picture shows Nathan Phillips Square and the area by Queen Street West and Bay Street. The Square is the most popular space of Toronto's downtown. Public meetings, markets, concerts, restaurants and just relaxing occur in the area around the central lake and fountain, which is transformed in winter months into an ice rink.

City Hall

In 1957, over 500 architects from around the world were invited to submit their ideas for Toronto's New City Hall. Architect Viljo Revell won this honour with his two curved towers of 27 and 22 storeys and a three storey 'Flying Saucer' that contains the City Council Chambers. September 13,1965 was opening day of the New City Hall and Nathan Phillips Square, named after the Toronto mayor who was responsible for the building's construction. The Square is home to the farmers market in summer months, hosts artists on weekends, and concerts and other artistic performances during the year, and has become the heart of Toronto.

Mackenzie House

The two-storey Georgian style stone townhouse of Toronto's first mayor and the leader of the 1837 Upper Canadian Rebellion, William Lyon Mackenzie, is located on Bond Street.

Western View

Just two centuries ago, the land around Bathurst Street was settled by a few hundred immigrants, and in 1793 the town of York was established. This evening picture was taken from Bathurst Street, where old Fort York is located.

Gardiner Expressway

The second picture was taken from Kippling Street bridge in Etobicoke and shows an important Toronto link, the Gardiner Expressway, with the city skyline in the background. 21 kilometres in length, the Expressway was constructed as an elevated freeway and provides convenient access to downtown Toronto.

King's Landing Marina

This morning picture was taken from King's Landing Marina, located near Queens Quay.

Downtown Parks

May is considered the nicest time in the city. Millions of tulips in public and private gardens dazzle everyone. Toronto is known as the city in the park. Hundreds of parks, large and small, are spread across the city, located in open spaces or squeezed between buildings in the business centre. Downtown parks are frequently used by locals during lunchtime. The larger parks around the city are fully occupied on weekends. The smaller picture shows popular Queens Park, full of big trees and flowers. In its southern part is the Ontario Parliament.

St. James Church

The Anglican cathedral, located by King Street East and Church Street, was built in 1853. Its 97 metre tall steeple, the tallest in Canada, was used to lead ships into the harbour. A charming garden surrounds the church. St. James Park, restored to 19-century horticultural style, is a cherished spot for weddings and a peaceful resting place for locals.

Toronto Weddings

Surrounding the St. James Cathedral, the park is sought out as a shady resting place for Torontonians working around downtown, and its gazebo is a favorite place for weddings in spring and summer months. Some 20,000 weddings are performed in Toronto yearly, one third of all Ontario's weddings. May 2002 brought a wedding day for this family, photographed in St James Park. In the background of the picture is St. Lawrence Hall.

Skyscrapers

Canada's largest banks are headquartered in the tallest skyscrapers along Bay and King Streets. 72 storeys of white marble is First Canadian Place, the tallest office building in Canada. Commerce Court has 57 storeys, Scotia Plaza with red–tinted trapeziod windows has 68 storeys, black–towered Toronto Dominion Centre has 56 storeys, Canada Trust Tower has 51 storeys and its second tower has 47 storeys. The CN Tower dwarfs them all at 553.33 metres. The Toronto Stock Exchange has only 49 storeys, but is one of the greatest in business value in North America. This picture was shot from Front Street.

Glass and Aluminium

The second photo shows skyscrapers around Bay and Front Streets.

Financial District

Toronto is a city on the go with a downtown core ever evolving into a more cosmopolitan and international urban centre. Despite the growing pains of big city density and traffic, downtown Toronto remains a friendly, easy place to explore. The Toronto-Dominion Centre, designed by Ludwig Miles van der Rohe, with its windy centre park is photographed on this page.

Downtown

This picture was taken from an airplane and shows the whole Toronto Downtown area from the south. Toronto's vigorous and unique architecture attracts not only tourists, but residents also walk with pleasure along the imposing mansions, old buildings and modern aluminium-glass office towers around Front Street West and Bay Street.

York University

York University, located on Steeles Avenue, was founded in 1959 with a class of 76 students. Now, the university offers 5000 courses in ten faculties yearly, offering the faculty of Enviromental Studies, Fine Art, Glendon College, Osgoode Hall Law school and more to thousands of students.

E. Turner Schoolhouse

Toronto's oldest surviving school, the Enoch Turner Schoolhouse was built in 1848 as the first free school in the young city. The school building, with a host of photographs and other memorabilia is occasionally open to the public. Restored classrooms are used for weddings and meetings.

Commerce Court

The financial centre of Canada, the largest in North America, employs 125,000 people in the finance sector. The Financial District is an area borderd by Front, John, Yonge and Dundas Streets. Commerce Court is located in the centre of this district, on King St. West. The building has 57 storeys and is 239 metres high. Its windy court space is a popular lunchtime rest area for workers. A statue of two businessmen by William McElcheran, called The Encounter, is placed in the assembly centre of the court.

SkyDome

Canada's greatest entertainment centre, Toronto's $500 million SkyDome opened in 1989. For concerts, there are seats for 67,000, and for sporting events there are seats for 45,000 spectators. The world's first fully retractable roof weighs 11,000 tons, and can be opened in 20 minutes. Two centre panels slide back and the end panel rotates 180 degrees under the first two. The architects of this project were Rod Robbie and Michael Allen. When the roof is open, a perfect view of the field can be had from the CN Tower. One could watch the game easily for no charge, however, the players are almost invisible from 477 metres up. The SkyDome is home to two sporting teams, the Toronto Blue Jays and the Toronto Argonauts. To help keep score, the Jumbotron Scoreboard is made of 420,000 light bulbs. The SkyDome can be seen from the outside as a violet glow on Toronto's night skyline. (page 43)

King St. – Bay St.

In the last thirty years, downtown Toronto has experienced unprecedented growth as massive developments on King Street West, Bay Street, Front Street, Harborfront and newly constructed buildings around SkyDome and the CN Tower continue to change the face of the city. On this page is a picture taken on King Street West, showing the Bank of Nova Scotia, Commerce Court and Canada Trust Tower. The second picture shows the view of the downtown skyscrapers, which you can see by turning your head or your camera's fisheye lens up to the sky. Toronto's downtown is a monumental place with massive buildings, very long streets and very tall towers. For taking distinctive pictures here, a fisheye lens on your camera is indispensable.

St. Michael's Cathedral

Built in Gothic style on Shuter and Bond Streets in Toronto's East York in 1848, St. Michael's is the principal church for Canada's largest English–speaking Catholic archdiocese. The architect W. Thomas was inspired by the 14th century Gothic Yorkminster in England. As well as huge stained-glass windows, the Cathedral also has a replica of Michelangelo's *Pieta*. This picture was taken during a mass in June.

St. John's Cemetery

One of the oldest cemeteries in the city, St. John's Cemetery Norway was established in 1853 on Kingston Street, in the eastern part of Toronto.

Campbell House

A fine example of Georgian architecture, this mansion located on Queen St. West and University Avenue, was built in 1822 for Judge William Campbell, chief justice of Upper Canada in 1825–1829. The house, located in a small, cozy garden, is open to the public.

Old City Hall

This is the third Old City Hall. The first one was destroyed by fire, the second City Hall was left for this Old City Hall. The second one was used from 1848–1899, and is used today as a part of the St. Lawrence Market (page 49). The Old City Hall was constructed from granite, delivered from the nearby Credit River, and from New Brunswick brownstone. A 90m clock tower crowns the City Hall, designed by J.M. Lennox and completed in 1899.

Royal York

Designed in the Beaux Arts contemporary style, Toronto's pre–eminent hotel is located on First Street in front of Union Station. The hotel was designed by Montreal architects Ross and Macdonald, and constructed in 1929. Local history began in 1843, when Captain Thomas Dick built the Ontario Terrace on this site. In 1853 the building was renamed 'Sword's Hotel' and later to 'Revere Hotel.' The present Royal York Hotel opened in 1929 with 1,048 rooms, the largest hotel kitchen in Canada and a Concert hall with a mammoth pipe organ weighing 50 tons. It was once the tallest building in the British Commonwealth. Royal York Hotel has welcomed over 40 million guests.

Dominion Public Building

Located on First St., the building was constructed in 1929 by Canada's Government in the grand Beaux-Arts style. The building was renovated in 1999.

Royal Bank Plaza

2,500 ounces of 24-carat gold was fused into the glass of 14,000 windows on both triangular Royal Bank Towers, located on Bay Street and Front Street. This building has more glass than any other skyscraper in the world, and each window contains about $70.00 worth of gold. In this picture is the south tower of 41 storeys, while the north tower has 26 storeys. On the left side of this picture is part of the Union Station facade.

Downtown Skyline

The second picture was taken from the south and shows the Toronto Downtown and Front Street. Union Station, the building with a green roof in front of the Royal York Hotel, is the largest and most opulent station built in Canada and one of the most significant hubs in Canadian transportation.

39

St. Lawrence Hall

Corinthian columns and a distinctive brass cupola are the identifying marks of this exquisite stone and iron historic building. St. Lawrence Hall, located on King Street East, served its first 75 years as the premier venue for public gatherings. In addition to St. Lawrence Hall and other buildings, Architect William Thomas designed nine churches in Toronto. The hall was restored in 1967 for Canada's centennial year.

Greektown

Tzatziki, souvlaki, baklava or other spicy Greek specialities are tasty reasons to visit Greektown, located along Danford Ave. Some bars and restaurants close late—early morning in the summer time. In the centre is placed a statue of the Greek conqueror, Alexander the Great, as shown in this picture. The third picture shows Danford Ave, the centre of Toronto's Greektown.

Trinity Church   FAR RIGHT >

In a cozy little shadowed square with a small pond just behind the north end of Eaton Centre is the Trinity Church.

Eaton Centre

Anything available in the world can be found in Toronto's biggest shopping mall, located by Yonge and Dundas. Its modern and light filled four-storey interior is home to hundreds of stores, boutiques and a food court. At the northwest corner of the mall is the Indigo book store. Tens of thousands of books, magazines, calendars, CDs and other products arranged on well-marked shelves attract shoppers to browse the meticulously organized store layout. Many authors hold signing sessions, giving fans an opportunity to meet their favourite writers. The in-store Indigo Café affords shoppers a place to sit and relax. Books which are not in stock can be ordered online at the computer kiosks. This largest national book retailer is a Canadian company and operates under the names of Indigo Books Music & more, Chapters, Coles, Smithbooks and World's Biggest Bookstore.

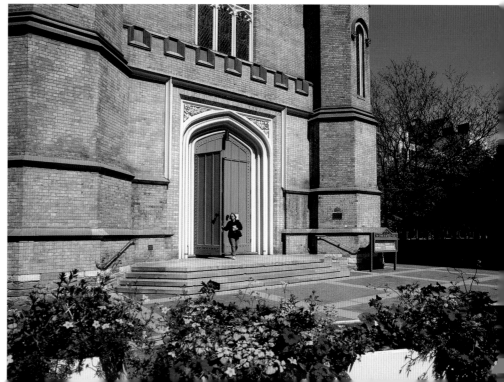

Theatres

The performing arts culture in Toronto is lively. Theatres, concert halls, ballet studios and movie theatres in Greater Toronto offer fine performances for those who enjoy the arts. Toronto is one of the three largest centres for live theatre in the English speaking world after New York and London. Hundreds of world–renowned artists perform every year in Toronto. Dozens of ballets, dramatic plays, world premieres of musicals and summer scenes are presented on the Harbourfront and in High Park, and are irresistible to locals and millions of tourists. Pictured on this page is the Canadian Opera Company's home, a renovated 19th century factory and warehouse building. Historic, beautifully reconstructed Royal Alexandra Theatre is in the second picture, producing world–famous musicals such as Jane Eyre or Mamma Mia. The National Ballet of Canada has its home in Toronto's Hummingbird Centre for the Performing Arts.

Night Panorama

When the sun falls behind the horizon and the city lights glimmer in a million points of light, the streets become the focus of cultural night life. Stage and movie theatres are full, bars and restaurants offer exotic menus complemented by nostalgic music from Toronto's jazz artists who perform nightly in the cafés. This nighttime panoramatic picture was taken from Centre Island.

Convention Centre

Metro Toronto Convention Centre is a busy meeting place, located on Front Street. The south entrance of the Centre is by Bremner St., close to the CN Tower and Skywalk, which connects the Union Station, Sky Dome and Front Street. In the front of the entrance, there are two sculptures of snowmen. In winter months, snowmen can be seen everywhere, but only Torontonians have iron, black, never-melting snowmen.

Festivals, Parades

Torontonians love special events, celebrations, parades and cultural traditions. Yonge and Bloor Streets are the right place for celebrations and parades. In summer months, Toronto Harbourfront, beaches, and parks boast numerous musical and theatre festivals, such as the Jazz Festival or Rhythms of the World. The Spadina Strawberry Festival is very popular. The Molson Indy attracts millions, not only from Ontario or Canada. The Toronto Outdoor Art Exhibition and Pride Toronto are both watched by hundreds of thousands.

Kensington Market   FAR RIGHT >

This flavourful area is located on Augusta and Oxford, by Spadina Avenue. Kensington Market, next to Chinatown, is heavily visited by tourists and locals. A special cheese delicatessen, vegetable and spice stores give the area a distinctive aroma.

Yonge Street

1886 km long Yonge St is considered the world's longest street, dividing Toronto west–east. Surveyed by Lt. Col. J.Simcoe, the street was named after Sir G. Yonge, British Minister of War. The street was once the commercial focus of Toronto in the 19th century. Now it is very popular with locals and tourists, and is the centre of shopping and small business. Yonge St. begins by Lake Ontario on Toronto Harbour, where Number One is the Toronto Star Building. After North York, Yonge leaves the city of Toronto and runs through Richmond Hill, Aurora, Newmarket and Holland Landing, where home numbers are over 20,000 at its end in Holland Marsh, a distance of 56 km from Toronto. In the past, Yonge St. was Hwy 11, and it ran through North Bay, Kapuskasing and Thunder Bay to the Rainy River on the US border. This is a distance of 1886 km from Toronto, and explains its distinction as the longest street in the world.

City Centre

Toronto's midtown is the area between Dundas, Front, Simcoe and Yonge Streets. This downtown view was taken from Simcoe Place. The tallest skyscraper in Toronto, and the tallest building in all of Canada is the 72-storey—tall, white—marbled First Canadian Place.

Richmond Street

A colourful landmark on Richmond Street is the modern Entertainment complex, with a Chapters Bookstore and Paramouth Cinemas, located in the Entertainment District, close to downtown.

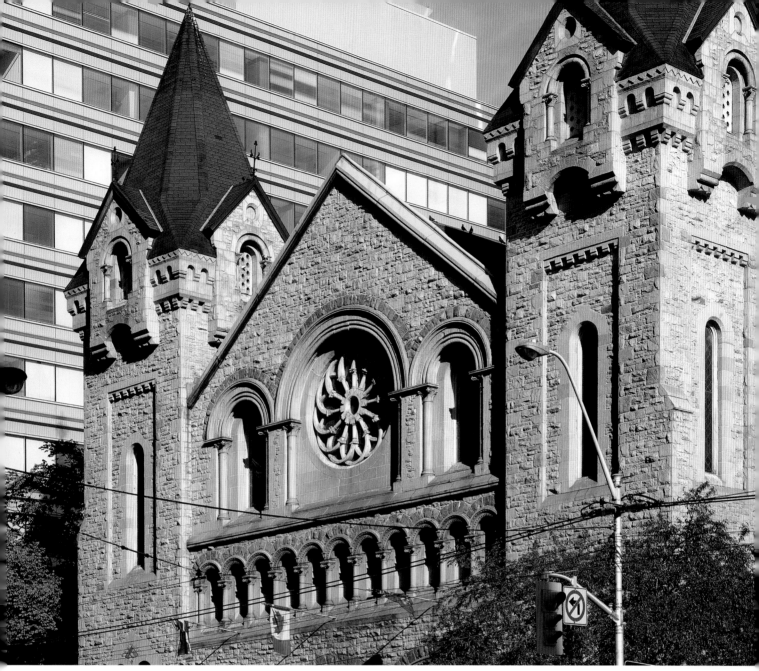

St. Andrew's

St. Andrew's Church, one of the oldest Presbyterian congregations in Canada, is a downtown oasis of silence and peace in the rushing financial world. The church is located by King and Simcoe Streets. The original church was founded in 1830 and the present building opened for worship in 1876. The church's choir has a tradition of providing fine music. A famous curiosity is its magnificent pipe organ with mechanical action. Beautiful concerts are performed at Christmas and Easter. The stone architecture of St. Andrew's contrasts beautifully with the modern aluminum and glass architecture of the tall buildings all around it.

100 Workers Memorial

A memorial to 100 Workers is located on Simcoe Place, by Front Street. The names of a hundred selected workers are written on the plaques, which are placed on the wall, in the picture.

Felician Sisters

This impressive Victorian house and well known architectural landmark, the Felician Sisters convent, is located on Augusta Street, just a step from Queen Street West.

Queen St. West

The centre of street life in Toronto is popular Queen Street West. Numerous small restaurants are busy all day, as young people, students and visitors browse the street markets. Cafés and ethnic restaurants are full of young Torontonians. Queen Street is an old Toronto street, where time in the summer seems to slow down.

Honest Ed's

This popular shopping centre, a part of the Mirvish Village, is located on the intersection of Bloor and Bathurst streets. Close neighbors are the Bathurst St. Theatre, Annex Theatre and Poor Alex Theatre.

Flat-Iron Mural

The 'Flat-Iron Mural' by Derek Besant is on the back side of the Gooderham Building. Some buildings in this area survived the Great Fire of 1904. The picture of the Gooderham building is on page 51.

St. Lawrence Market

Since 1901, the St. Lawrence Market has been known primarily for its fruit, cheese, meat, fish and vegetables. When Market Gallery opened in 1979, people realized that the civic chamber of Toronto's 1845 City Hall still remained enclosed within the market. This nearly forgotten treasure now offers a variety of exhibitions including historic and current paintings, photographs and the other items which explore the art, culture and history of Toronto. An interesting feature is the City Hall stone entrance, still visible in the front of the Market which was built later.

Galleria

Spanish architect and sculptor Santiago Calatrava designed this magnificent steel–glass canopy, which creates a ground-level atrium that includes the reconstructed Midland Commercial Bank building. The Galleria and BCE Place, the second most distinctive spot in Toronto, are located on Bay Street.

The Hockey Hall of Fame

A popular tourist stop is The Hockey Hall of Fame, located on Front Avenue, close to the Dominion Public Building. The Hall building is shown in the second picture on this page.

Gooderham Building

The romance of a golden age surrounds you as you walk along the oldest part of Front Street. A wedge–shaped Victorian landmark located in the centre of the St. Lawrence district, the Gooderham Building is—along with the CN Tower—the most photographed city landmark. The building, which is nicknamed the Flat-Iron Building, was built in 1892 for financier George Gooderham. The picture of the Flat-Iron Mural from Derek Besant, placed on the back wall of the building, is on page 49.

City Artists

The focal point of Toronto artists is the St. Lawrence district, one of the oldest areas in Toronto. Its centre, Front Street, is lined with attractive stores, art boutiques and restaurants. On Saturday, different artists display paintings and sculptures, as in this picture, taken at the St. Lawrence Market.

Megacity

Over 100 ethnic communities live in the city of Greater Toronto, created in 1997 when the older suburban municipalities of East York, Scarborough, Etobicoke and North York were merged with Toronto and a megacity of 4.9 million people was born. Toronto, whose history dates back to 1615, now has a university, hundreds of theatres, libraries, concert halls, galleries and museums. Some statistics show that, for instance, 80,000 immigrants came to Toronto from 160 countries in just one year (1997 year calculation); 48% of Toronto's population are immigrants; one third of Canada's population lives within a 160 km radius from Toronto; 4000 people per square km live in Toronto and 20,000 marriages are performed annually in Greater Toronto. 21 million tourists and visitors arrive in Toronto each year, mostly via the international airport, 2 million of them visit the CN Tower and 15 million travel to Niagara.

Simcoe Place

A favoured quiet spot in the busy downtown is a park between King, Wellington, John and Simcoe Streets. This park is home to St. Andrew's Church, Roy Thomson Hall, Metro Centre and The Memorial of 100 workers. The CBC Broadcast Centre is located close by, just across Wellington Street.

Roy Thomson Hall

Designed by architect Arthur Erickson, Roy Thomson Hall is home to the Toronto Symphony Orchestra. The hall, located on King and Simcoe Streets, was completed in 1982 as a part of the famous Massey Hall. Toronto has dozens of instrumental groups. The Baroque Orchestra Taffelmusic offers music from Mozart, Vivaldi, Handel and more. Hundreds of world renowned artists and singers perform in the Roy Thomson and Massey Halls yearly, with many orchestras and famous guest conductors.

53

Stock Exchange

TSX Group has been the heart of Canada's capital market for 150 years. Located on York and King Streets, the Toronto Stock Exchange, well known as TSX, has become one of the larger world financial institutions. The Group offers two conference centres, Stock Market Place and The Executive Boardroom with a 24 person capacity—ideal for presentations, press conferences, teleconferences, distance learning or smaller private working sessions. The Boardroom is equipped with two plasma screens, an LCD projector and broadcast quality lighting. Stock Market Place is the visitor and media centre where news media interview leading financial experts and broadcast financial news. Stock Market Place is fully equipped as a high-tech event venue for meetings, receptions or media announcements. The first picture shows the building, and the second photograph was taken in Stock Market Place.

Aerial View

Founded in 1793 with about 200 residents, in just over two centuries, the city has grown into Canada's largest city with citizens from all over the world. Early residents arrived with hope for a peaceful life. They started as farmers and built small mills and farmhouses. The small city of York was incorporated into the 10,000–strong city of Toronto in 1834. By the end of the 19th century, the population reached 200,000. Farmhouses were moved out of the city centre, the mills were closed and old buildings demolished. New buildings and factories were erected and Toronto became the centre of trade and industry in Canada.

Churchill Memorial

An imposing statue of a Canadian friend, the British Prime Minister Sir Winston Churchill, can be found in the south-western corner of Nathan Phillips Square.

Inner Harbour

Sailing around Toronto Harbour on the open lake is a pleasing experience. On a sunny spring day, one can see Toronto's spectacular skyline.

Toronto Islands

There are thirteen small and large islands in Toronto's Inner Harbour. The three largest are connected to Toronto by ferry. Ward's Island, on the left side of the picture, is mostly a residential area with a beach on its southern side. Centre Island and Olympic Island are heavily visited on the weekends by thousands of Torontonians. Hanlan's Island has a beautiful park and a long beach on its south side. All of the largest and more important islands are connected by bridges and paths. This picture was taken on Centre Island.

Queen's Quay

Old chartered boats, moored private boats, Toronto Police Marine vessels, and Toronto Fire Department vessels, the SkyDome, the CN Tower, high apartment buildings, and the decorative stones on Queen's Quay Street are all neighbours to Harbourfront Park.

Queen's Quay Terminal

Harbourfront is a place for Sunday markets. An assortment of artwork, antiques, gift shops, bookstores, and more attract those who like to browse around the piers, boats and small stores. For those who love music, dancing, theatre, or ethnic festivals, Harbourfront is the ideal place from spring to fall. A popular local spot is Queen's Quay Terminal, seen in the second picture.

Western Channel

The Western Channel, the entrance to the Toronto Innner Harbour, looks like an ocean shore.

City Centre Airport

War planes from the Canadian Warplane Heritage Museum— located close to Toronto in Hamilton—are ocassionally displayed at the Toronto City Centre Airport. The Terminal 'A' building is one of several long–surviving air terminals in Canada. The airport is connected with the city via ferry from lower Bathurst Street. This picture was taken during the 'Doors Open Toronto' civic event.

Toronto Port

The Port of Toronto is located close to downtown, and can be reached via Parliament and Cherry Streets. Clark Beach Park and North Shore Park, popular recreational destinations, are located on the south side of this area.

Harbour Square

The centre of Toronto's harbourfront is Harbour Square and in its centre is Queen's Quay Terminal. Large chartered boats are moored in York Street Slip, around the hotels and piers. Harbour Square is heavily visited in summer months. Moored charter boats and historic vessels attract visitors to sail Toronto's inner harbour, or down Lake Ontario to Niagara Falls. The second picture, taken from the CN Tower, shows Union Station, the Gardiner Expressway, the port, and Toronto's islands.

CN Tower

The $63 million (1976 figure) CN Tower was completed in 1976 after 40 months of construction by 1537 workers. The World's Tallest Building and Free Standing Structure weighs 130,000 tons and its construction called for 53,000 cubic yards of concrete. The CN Tower is one of the seven wonders of the modern world. The CN Tower was designed by architect John Andrews. The Glass Floor is popular with tourists. Although the Glass Floor is designed to cary the weight of 14 large hippos, walking on it is a chilling experience.

Growing City

Toronto is a city on the go. There are hundreds of new constructions in the downtown area, and the streets are growing and changing. In the lower picture, the CN Tower seems to be posed by a crane. This is just a camera joke. The construction of the tower was in reality much more complicated.

The World's Tallest

Two million annual visitors are lifted to the tower Sphere and SkyPod by six glass-fronted, high-speed elevators. The CN Tower looks like a huge space ship from the ground, shot from a short distance by a fish eye lens. The tower is 533.33 metres tall, but the highest point for visitors is the SkyPod, 477m above the ground, costing some $25 admission to reach it. In comparison, helicopter trips are more expensive. A six minute flight costs almost one hundred dollars for three passengers. Photographic trips are yet more expensive, one hour in a helicopter costs from one to three thousand dollars, but flights are safe and very quiet. Three flights were needed to complete this book.

Torontonians

The true builders of the city are the working people. Proud of their city, Torontonians have worked to make the city beautiful and prosperous.

Scarborough

New and attractively designed apartment buildings, with 25 or more storeys are everywhere around Greater Toronto. This picture was taken by Progress Avenue, near Scarborough Town Centre.

Cornell House

The Scarborough Historical Museum is located in the beautiful grounds of Thomson Memorial Park in Cornell House on Birmley Road. The McCowan log house, Kennedy Discovery Gallery and Houg Carriage Works are alongside. The complex of village buildings was built in 1850–1858.

Toronto Designers

A long line of architects designed the city of Toronto buildings and interiors through the years. There are many names and buildings—E.J. Lennox's Old City Hall was replaced by Viljo Revel's new City Hall, I.M. Pei designed Commerce Court, the red tinted stone of the Scotia Plaza design was created by WZMH Architects and John Andrews is an architect of the CN Tower. Edward Durell is responsible for the 290m First Canadian Place–the tallest Canadian office building, The Toronto-Dominion Centre was designed by Ludwig Miles van der Rohe and the 26 and 41-story twin tower, gold mirrored Royal Bank Plaza by Boris Zerafa. Rod Robbie and Michael Allen designed the phenomenal SkyDome.

Bremner Blvd.

The area of Bremner Blvd. is fairly quiet. A small park, the Skywalk and downtown are the focus of this picture.

Scarborough Centre

The modern architecture of Canada Centre building is captured in the above picture. The Scarborough Civic Centre in the second picture was designed by architect Raymond Moriyama. The area around the administrative centre is a lively meeting place for musicians, wedding parties, politicans and tourists.

Scarborough Bluffs

90 metres above Lake Ontario rises Scarborough Bluffs, created millions years ago by receding glaciers. Challenging trails will lead tourists along beautiful parts of the Scarborough lake front. Several recreational sites with hotels, restaurants and marinas attract people year-round.

Toronto's Zoo

One of the largest in the world, Metro Toronto Zoo is popular among children and adults. Located in Scarborough's Rouge River valley, the zoo was designed by architect Raymond Moriyama in an African Safari style. Over 4000 animals are spread freely in the wide area and in eight glass-roofed pavilions. The zoo is visited not only by families and school trips, but thousands of retired citizens with annual tickets use the zoo as a park.

Wild Water Kingdom

Wild Water Kingdom is heavily used in hot summer days. It is Canada's largest outdoor water park. Located north of Toronto in Brampton, the park can be easily reached via Steeles Avenue or Finch Avenue.

Canada's Wonderland

The entrance part of Canada's premier theme park, named 'Paramount Canada's Wonderland' is photographed in the second picture. The Park offers over 200 attractions to families. An excellent selection of roller coasters, and a 20–acre water park are the most popular attractions. The park is located north of Toronto, in Vaugham, and can be reached via Highway 400.

Richmond Hill

Richard Vanderburg, a hero of the American Revolutionary War settled here, in today's Richmond Hill in 1833, and built this fine clapboard house in the Georgian architectural tradition. Richmond Hill, Toronto's close neighbour, is the home of the David Dunlop Observatory, photographed on page 73.

North York

North York City Centre and Yonge St. by Silver City are the subjects of the second picture.

The Gibson House

In time, Torontonians came to appreciate their past and saved some of the city's historical buildings and farms. They have been restored to their original condition, beautifully conveying the architecture and design of their days, some preserved as museums. The farmhouse of rebel, politician and surveyor David Gibson is located in North York on Yonge Street. The Gibson family home, a red-brick Georgian–style house built in 1851 now serves as a museum.

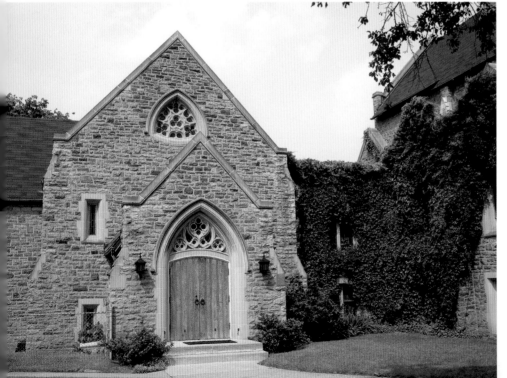

Port Credit

Mississauga's gate to Lake Ontario is Port Credit. A park and several marinas by the lake are favoured recreational spots with restaurants, fishing cruises and hundreds of moored boats. Mississauga, one of Canada's fastest growing cities, absorbed several villages including Port Credit and Streetsville. A well known spot in the city centre is the Mississauga Civic Centre, located on Hurontario Street.

Islington Church

A landmark at the centre of Islington Village, the Islington United Church, in the second picture, was first built in 1834. The present building, designed by architects Bruce, Brown and Brisley, was built of Ontario sandstone and was consecrated in 1949. The Church House in the picture was completed in 1955.

Chinese Centre

The Mississauga Chinese Centre draws shoppers with its Nine–Dragon Wall. It is the only one of its kind outside of Asia. The Dragon Wall is used by the ruling family as a barrier in their gardens and only the Emperor may have nine dragons on the wall. The second picture shows the gift of Jinagsu Provincial Government, called the 'Pavillon of Friendship.'

Mississauga

Toronto's close neighbour, Mississauga, is located on the Lake Ontario shore, just east of Etobicoke.

Toronto Airport

1100 aircraft land and depart daily from Toronto's Lester B. Pearson Internatioinal Airport. This busy airport welcomes 28 million passengers yearly at its three terminals. The maximum hourly airport capacity is 50 flights. 50 airlines operate out of LBPIA, situated on 1,792 hectares. The airport, which employs 17,000 workers, is connected with Toronto's downtown by the public city transport, TTC. Bus line 192, called the 'Airport Rocket,' moves travellers and employees to the Kippling Subway Station in about 20 minutes for a regular transport charge of $2.25. From here, passengers can easily reach any location in Greater Toronto. Some seventy Subway stations over three lines are connected by a network of streetcars and buses. The first picture shows an aircraft takeoff, and the second was taken in Terminal 3.

Pioneer Village

In Black Creek Pioneer Village in northern Toronto, the life and times of rural Ontario of the 19th century will surround you. 40 restored buildings with actors in period dresses, farms with animals, and a water mill will charm visitors of this historic village. It is a very popular place for family and school tours.

Todmorden Mills

Toronto's early industry is found within Todmorden Mills, setted in the Don River Valley. In 1794, Isaiah and Aaron Skinner built a sawmill and grist–mill near this site. By 1823 Thomas Helliwell had built a brewery and distillery in the immediate vicinity, and several years later, a second paper mill was constructed by Skinner and Eastwood. A century ago, mills provided flour, bricks, lumber, paper, beer and whiskey to a growing Toronto. Today the Arts Centre provides visual and performing arts here.

York

The history of York began early in the 18th century when J.G. Simcoe founded Fort York. In 1812, only 700 people lived in the area, which twice was invaded by Americans. Over the next few decades, thousands of British immigrants moved to this city.

Scadding Cabin

The oldest building in Toronto, the old cabin in the second picture, was built on the east bank of the Don River in 1794 for John Scadding, the clerk to Lieutenant-Governor John Graves Simcoe. Later, in 1879, the cabin was moved to the CNE site by the York Pioneer and Historical Society. The cabin is open to the public during the CNE, and is located in the southern part, close to Fort Rouillé (page 4).

Science in Toronto

The largest optical telescope in Canada is housed under the roof of the David Dunlop Observatory in Richmond Hill. The observatory, which is part of the University of Toronto, is open on clear evenings to the public. Another educational place is the Ontario Science Centre, one of Toronto's more popular science sites, where almost 800 interactive exhibits attract thousands of visitors daily. Science demonstrations and programs are a great family activity. One million people visit the Centre yearly, which was designed by Vancouver–born architect R. Moriyama. The centre, organized by theme, is described as a vast playground of science.

Filtration Plant

The R.C. Harris Filtration Plant, located on the hill by the eastern end of the Beaches Park, looks like a castle. However, this *castle* produces clean drinking water for millions.

Allan Gardens

Palm House and six greenhouses fill 16,000 square feet with colorful tropical and subtropical plants. Palm House is centered in Allan Gardens, renamed after its founder George W. Allan, who donated five acres to the Toronto Horticultural Society in 1858. Allan Gardens are located by Carlton and Sherbourne Streets. The Toronto Horticultural Society was founded in 1834 by Sir J. Colborne, the Governor of Upper Canada. Allan Gardens, originally named 'The Horticultural Gardens' was opened in 1860 by Edward VII. Additional land was added to the garden in 1864. Later, in 1901, the park was renamed to "Allan Gardens."

Spadina Gardens

The Queens Quay along Lower Spadina Avenue is a lovely living area. This evening picture shows Spadina Quay marina and Harbourfront Park.

Panorama

Riverdale Park and Don Valley are regular weekend family destinations. The soccer field is usually occupied, and the area by Riverdale Hospital is used for Sunday Markets and picnics. The Don Valley park slopes, occupied by dozing and sunbathing people, offer a beautiful view of the downtown skyscrapers and CN Tower to numerous photographers and painters.

Don Valley Parkway

The Don Valley Parkway is a favourite course for Toronto's Sunday cyclists. A thousand cyclists enjoy the smooth concrete surface of the 14-kilometre–long highway. 150 years ago, nearby Todmorden Mills and Don Valley Brick Works were major suppliers of bricks and other building material to the builders of the young and growing city of Toronto.

Hanlan's Island

Three Toronto island ports are connected via the city ferry, which travels to each island's port every 30 minutes from early morning to late evening. While Ward Island is mostly residential, Centre and Hanlan's Islands are open for recreation. The history of Hanlan's Island begins in 1843, when the Privat Brothers opened a small amusement park on Toronto Island. This park was the first in Ontario. Later in the 1880s, N. Hanlan and L. Solman opened another amusement park, equipped with a carousel, shooting galleries, a scenic railway, a dance pavillion, a large hotel and a museum of living curiosities. The park was damaged by fire in 1909 and reopened one year later.

Point Gibraltar

This Historic lighthouse is 100 feet tall, and is located deep on the south side of Hanlan's Island.

477m above the Earth

There is no higher building on Earth where a person can stand and overlook an entire city as do these two American tourists. The Skypod, on the CN Tower in Toronto, is 477 metres above the ground. On a clear day, Niagara Falls can be seen from here. The CN Tower measures 553.33 metres, including antennas. World architects are still reaching higher and higher with daring projects…but Canada's CN Tower is still the tallest.

Toronto Photos

In numerous pictures in this book, the CN Tower is visible. I wished to take some pictures without this Toronto landmark, but met with little success—the Tower is visible from everywhere. It's just so terribly tall…

Waterfront

Lake Ontario is real playground for Torontonians, and this picture clearly shows the city's ideal location. Large hotels stand just metres from the lake shore, and recreational boats are moored at numerous marinas right under apartment buildings. Three ferry lines connect all islands, where numerous marinas, family playgrounds, beaches and ports invite thousands of visitors daily. The most frequently visited are Centre and Hanland's Islands.

Ontario Place

Three man–made islands are home to Ontario Place, an internationally acclaimed cultural, leisure and entertainment parkland. The 96 acre site was first opened to the public in May of 1971. A Cinesphere with an 80x60' screen, a South Beach volleyball complex, a Soak City waterpark, and concerts with popular singers are irresistible to summer visitors. The aerial picture shows the whole island, located by Lakeshore Blvd West. The Exhibition Place and the Toronto City Centre Airport are nearby.

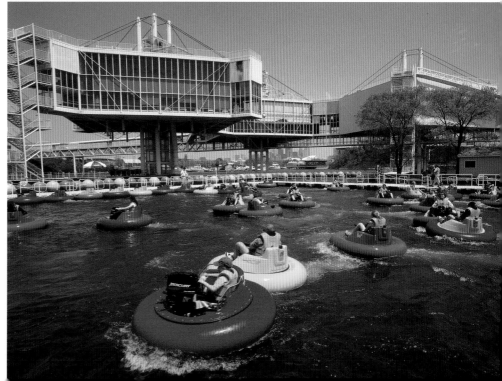

KEW Gardens

Summer is usually very hot in Toronto, so gardens and beaches are full of people looking for shady places and fresh water. A frequent weekend destination are the KEW Gardens. Close by are KEW Beach, Beaches Park and Balmy Beach, located near the R.C.Harris Filtration Plant, east of downtown. Several kilometres of clean sand and warm water, a path for cyclists, pedestrians and roller bladers, a park and a pool attract thousands daily. All the lovely beaches around Toronto are without any admission fees. Eastern Beaches has a history dating back to the 1880's, when Victoria Park, financed by several prominent citizens, opened with numerous attractions, on today's Victoria Park Avenue. A small amusement park named Scarborough Beach Park opened in 1907 and five years later, the Toronto Railway Company expanded the park facilities.

Toronto Beaches

The rain, snow and cold of winter is fast forgotten in May, as the sun calls Torontonians to the lake shores. Lake Ontario offers kilometres of beautiful, sandy beaches around Toronto, Scarborough and Mississauga. Beaches Park is located east of downtown. For those who want to be on the beach free of swimsuits, the best place is a beach on Hanlan's Island, which can be reached by city ferry in minutes for $5. Popular Sunnyside Beach offers beaches with a trail and occasionally with free concerts. Wild beaches full of birds and with long trails for cyclists go around Tommy Thompson Park and by Leslie Street Spit, which is open to the public only on weekends. Private transport is not allowed, as there are shuttles to transport visitors free of charge. Waterfront Trail offers kilometres of enjoyable walking from Humber Bay Park to the Eastern Beach.

High Park

This largest Toronto park was founded in 1873 by J.G. Howard and his wife. The Howards lived here in 1855, and they were concerned about the lack of healthy recreational opportunities for the citizens of Toronto. The Howards deeded their property to the City of Toronto in 1873 for use as a public park. High Park quickly became the favourite weekend destination of Torontonians. The park's hills are fully occupied on hot days, the picnic area by the small zoo is a popular place for families, and seniors enjoy flowers and quiet shady gardens. Concerts and theatres are performed here in summer months.

Humber Valley

Etienne Brule Park and Old Mill Bridge, along with Humber River are shown in this picture. The Humber River has a good stock of Rainbow Trout, Smallmouth Bass, and Chinook Salmon.

Highway 401

The busiest Canadian highway begins in Windsor and runs through southern Ontario to Toronto. Together with the Macdonald–Cartier Freeway, it creates eight traffic lanes each way, and later continues to Kingston and Québec, where it becomes Hwy 20. Highway 401 is 900 km long. This picture was taken during morning rush hour from the Islington Street bridge.

Commission Building

The second picture shows the historic Toronto Harbour Commission Building, built in 1917 in Beaux Arts style. The building was originally built on the shore of Lake Ontario, but the lakeshore filling in 1920 extended the land southward, leaving the Commission Building far away from the lake.

Humber Bay

Overlooked from the tower, Lake Ontario's Humber Bay seems like an ocean. The westernmost part of Centre Island, with the City Centre Airport, is an important hub for Toronto business.

Music Garden

Walking along the Harbourfront from Bathurst Street via Queen's Quay to lower Yonge Street where ferry terminals connect Toronto with its Islands, one will see the whole harbourfront area, its parks, views of the CN Tower, and the SkyDome. Toronto Harbourfront is a great place not only for watersport lovers and tourists, but is a beautiful and exclusive living area. Some apartments and penthouses can be bought for about two or three million dollars. Apartment buildings, the Music Garden and Spadina Quay with the CN Tower in the background are shown in the small picture.

Exhibition Place

Lake Shore Blvd is home to Exhibition Place, open since 1879. The CNE attracts visitors from August through Labour Day, but numerous other events in the National Trade Centre, the Automotive Building, and the Sports Hall attract visitors throughout the year. Exhibition Place is a venue to more than 100 special events, consumer and trade shows. 4 to 5 million visitors visit the 192–acre site annually. The Molson Indy, International Boat Show, Sportsman's Show and Home Improvement Show are well attended. The first picture shows the Beaux Arts Pavillon Horticulture Building. At its front are stone sculptures of Roman and Greek Gods. Pictured is "Pan," the elusive god of the forest, half man and half goat. The National Trade Centre and Princes' Gates are in the two smaller pictures. Other attractions are Fort Rouillé, the French post and Scadding Cabin, the oldest house in Toronto. Both are located in the southern part of Exhibition Place. Pictures are on page 4 and 72.

Lake Ontario

The third largest in Canada, Lake Ontario is a playground for locals and visitors, and is an important transportation link. The Harbourfront is a favoured recreational place, with boats moored in numerous docks, always ready for fishing or sailing. In the bottom of the frame, Bathurst Street and Alexandra Park are visible.

Trips to Niagara

Chartered trips around Toronto's Islands or far into Lake Ontario on classic historic boats or on modern superfast ships are a draw for tourists. Lake trips to Niagara Falls are popular, and can be boarded on the Harbourfront. The Seaflight Hydrofoils vessel in the second picture connects Toronto's Harbourfront Park with Niagara Falls via the lake. The falls are reached in 90 minutes, with a lovely lake experience in summer months, or in winter by bus for very reasonable prices.

Niagara Falls

Canada's most visited attraction, Niagara Falls and the area around, called the 'Golden Horseshoe', receives over 18 million visitors annually. Niagara Falls is one of the seven wonders of the world and is the world's largest waterfall, with 3 million litres of crystal clear water falling every second through the falls. The first person to successfully go over the falls in a barrel was schoolteacher Anna Taylor in 1901. The Canadian falls, named 'Horseshoe Falls' for their shape, are 800m wide and 50m high.

Welland Canal

A busy part of the St. Lawrence Seaway, Welland Canal links Lakes Ontario and Erie for thousands of commercial ships. The first canal was completed in 1829. The present canal, the third, has served since 1932. For more local or Eastern Canada photographs, please refer to our line of books ONTARIO, CANADA and ATLANTIC CANADA.

About the Photographer

The author of this book, photographer Josef Hanus, owner of JH.Fine Art Photo Ltd., is one of the most accredited and celebrated scenery and wilderness photographers in Canada and North America. He has created, including photography and publishing, over 10 photographic tourist books and over 70 different Canadian calendars since 1989. Now he is working on a long line of new photographic books with the theme he loves the most—Canada. His award winning photographs and best selling Canadian calendars and photographic books come from hard work. After graduating from Art and Photography University in Europe, he has published thousands of photographs and articles in magazines and newspapers and continues observing nature through his camera lens. Studying objects, he trained his taste for scenic views and his eye to the height of artistic professionalism. But his sensitive sight is not the only source of success. Over the years, he has perfectly selected his professional partners and patiently tested cameras and film for his high quality work. The result of this effort can be seen in his products. People love his photographic books and calendars because Josef loves to create them. Since 1997, he has been working with his son, Josef M. Hanus.

About the Heart—JH.Fine Art Photo's published products are visibly marked with Josef's trademark, a red heart combined with Canada's maple leaf.